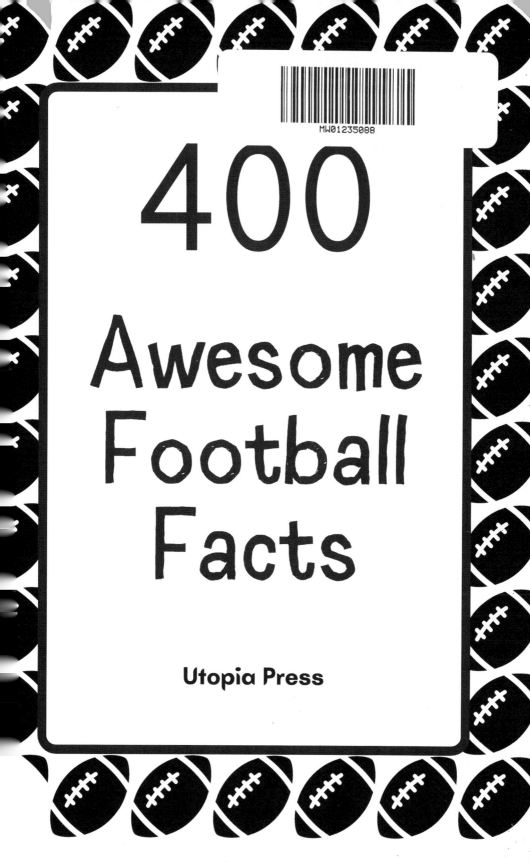

400

Awesome Football Facts

Utopia Press

The National Football League (NFL) first begun in 1920

The Green Bay Packers are the oldest founded team in the NFL, established in 1919

In 1967, the NFL had its first Super Bowl

The Pittsburgh Steelers and the New England Patriots have the record for the most Super Bowl wins at six each

The Cleveland Browns have the most NFL championships, with eight wins before the Super Bowl era

---

The Chicago Bears have the most retired jersey numbers in the NFL, with 14

The Baltimore Ravens were previously the Cleveland Browns until they relocated in 1996

The Dallas Cowboys have the highest overall winning percentage in NFL history

The Miami Dolphins achieved the only perfect season in NFL history in 1972, going 17-0

The New York Jets won Super Bowl III, led by quarterback Joe Namath

Tom Brady holds the record for the most Super Bowl wins by a player, with seven

Jerry Rice is the all-time leader in receiving yards in the NFL

Emmitt Smith is the all-time leader in rushing yards in the NFL

Peyton Manning has the most career passing touchdowns in NFL history

Brett Favre holds the record for the most career interceptions thrown

The longest field goal in NFL history was kicked by Matt Prater, who made a 64-yarder in 2013

The most points scored by a team in a single game is 72, accomplished by the Washington Redskins in 1940

The Cleveland Browns have the longest active playoff drought, not making the playoffs since 2002

The Chicago Bears have the most Hall of Fame inductees in NFL history

The New England Patriots had a perfect regular season in 2007, going 16-0

The Buffalo Bills appeared in four consecutive Super Bowls from 1991 to 1994 but failed to win any of them

The New York Giants have won the Super Bowl four times, all of them with quarterback Eli Manning

The Pittsburgh Steelers have won the most Super Bowls with different starting quarterbacks

The NFL implemented a salary cap system in 1994 to promote competitive balance

The New Orleans Saints' first playoff win in franchise history came in 2000

The Oakland Raiders have moved cities multiple times, starting in Oakland, then moving to Los Angeles, and then back to Oakland

The Philadelphia Eagles won their first Super Bowl in 2018, defeating the New England Patriots

The Houston Texans joined the NFL as an expansion team in 2002

The Atlanta Falcons lost to the Patriots in Super Bowl LI after leading by 25 points in the third quarter

The NFL has a total of 32 teams, divided into two conferences: the NFC and the AFC

The Vince Lombardi Trophy is awarded to the winner of the Super Bowl

The Pro Football Hall of Fame is located in Canton, Ohio

The NFL Draft is held annually to allocate new players to teams

The Detroit Lions have never appeared in a Super Bowl

The Kansas City Chiefs won their first Super Bowl in 50 years in 2020

The Seattle Seahawks won their first Super Bowl in 2014, defeating the Denver Broncos

The Minnesota Vikings have the most conference championship appearances without a Super Bowl win (four)

The Denver Broncos won back-to-back Super Bowls in 1998 and 1999

The Tampa Bay Buccaneers won their second Super Bowl in 2021, defeating the Kansas City Chiefs

The San Francisco 49ers have won the most conference championships, with 7

The New York Jets' only Super Bowl appearance and victory came in Super Bowl III

The Indianapolis Colts relocated from Baltimore to Indianapolis in 1984

The Arizona Cardinals are the oldest continuously run professional football team in the United States

The New Orleans Saints won their first Super Bowl in 2010, defeating the Indianapolis Colts

The Miami Dolphins had the only undefeated season in NFL history

The Jacksonville Jaguars and the Carolina Panthers joined the NFL as expansion teams in 1995

The Los Angeles Rams have relocated multiple times, moving from Cleveland to Los Angeles, then to St. Louis, and finally back to Los Angeles

The Cincinnati Bengals have never won a Super Bowl

The Washington Football Team was previously known as the Washington Redskins until 2020

The Tennessee Titans were previously the Houston Oilers until they relocated in 1997

The Kansas City Chiefs won their first Super Bowl in Super Bowl IV

The Green Bay Packers won the first two Super Bowls in 1967 and 1968

The Buffalo Bills made it to four consecutive Super Bowls from 1990 to 1993 but lost all of them

The Dallas Cowboys won three Super Bowls in the 1990s

The New England Patriots had a dynasty in the 2000s, winning six Super Bowls

The Philadelphia Eagles won their first Super Bowl in 2018

The Pittsburgh Steelers have won the most Super Bowls, with six titles

The San Francisco 49ers had a dynasty in the 1980s and 1990s, winning five Super Bowls

The New York Giants have won four Super Bowls, all under different head coaches

The Denver Broncos have won three Super Bowls

The Oakland Raiders have won three Super Bowls

The Arizona Cardinals have never won a Super Bowl

The Cincinnati Bengals have never won a Super Bowl

The Dallas Cowboys have appeared in the most Super Bowls, with eight appearances

The New England Patriots have appeared in the second-most Super Bowls, with eleven appearances

The Pittsburgh Steelers have appeared in the third-most Super Bowls, with eight appearances.

The Buffalo Bills have appeared in four consecutive Super Bowls

The Dallas Cowboys have won the most division titles, with 24

The Pittsburgh Steelers have won the second-most division titles, with 23

The Dallas Cowboys have the most playoff appearances, with 34

The Pittsburgh Steelers have the second-most playoff appearances, with 33

The Dallas Cowboys have the most playoff wins, with 35

The Dallas Cowboys have the highest all-time winning percentage, with .572

The Green Bay Packers have the second-highest all-time winning percentage, with .567

The Chicago Bears have the third-highest all-time winning percentage, with .565

The Arizona Cardinals have the third-lowest all-time winning percentage, with .420

The Cleveland Browns have the most losing seasons, with 29

The Arizona Cardinals have the second-most losing seasons, with 27

The Detroit Lions have the third-most losing seasons, with 26

The Dallas Cowboys have the most consecutive winning seasons, with 20 from 1966 to 1985

The New England Patriots have the second-most consecutive winning seasons, with 19 from 2001 to 2019

The San Francisco 49ers have the third-most consecutive winning seasons, with 16 from 1983 to 1998

The Miami Dolphins had the longest winning streak in NFL history, winning 17 consecutive games in the 1972-1973 season

The New England Patriots had the longest winning streak in the regular season, winning 21 consecutive games from 2003 to 2004

The Tampa Bay Buccaneers had the longest losing streak in NFL history, losing 26 consecutive games from 1976 to 1977

The Chicago Bears have the most regular-season wins in NFL history, with 790 wins

The Green Bay Packers have the second-most regular-season wins, with 778 wins

The New York Giants have the third-most regular-season wins, with 686 wins

The Chicago Bears have the most ties in NFL history, with 42 ties

---

The Green Bay Packers have the second-most ties, with 40 ties

---

The Dallas Cowboys have the most playoff appearances without a losing season, with 33 playoff appearances and no losing seasons

---

The San Francisco 49ers have the second-most playoff appearances without a losing season, with 27 playoff appearances and no losing seasons

The Indianapolis Colts have the third-most playoff appearances without a losing season, with 28 playoff appearances and no losing seasons

The Denver Broncos have the most Super Bowl losses, with five

The Buffalo Bills have the most consecutive Super Bowl losses, losing four consecutive Super Bowls from 1991 to 1994

The New England Patriots have the most Super Bowl appearances, with eleven

The Pittsburgh Steelers have the second-most Super Bowl appearances, with eight

The New England Patriots have the most consecutive Super Bowl appearances, appearing in three consecutive Super Bowls from 2017 to 2019

The Pittsburgh Steelers have the second-most consecutive Super Bowl appearances, appearing in three consecutive Super Bowls twice (1974-1976 and 1978-1980

The New England Patriots have the most consecutive playoff appearances, making the playoffs for 11 consecutive seasons from 2009 to 2019

The San Francisco 49ers have the second-longest home winning streak, winning 18 consecutive home games from 1988 to 1990

The New England Patriots have the longest home winning streak, winning 21 consecutive home games from 2002 to 2005

The Green Bay Packers have the most NFL championships, with 13 championships before the Super Bowl era

The Pittsburgh Steelers have the most playoff wins by a head coach, with 36 playoff wins under head coach Chuck Noll

The New England Patriots have the second-most playoff wins by a head coach, with 31 playoff wins under head coach Bill Belichick

---

Charles Haley has the second-most Super Bowl wins by a player, with five Super Bowl victories

---

Joe Montana and Terry Bradshaw have the third-most Super Bowl wins by a player, with four Super Bowl victories each

---

Tom Brady has the most Super Bowl appearances by a player, with ten Super Bowl appearances

Adam Vinatieri has the most career points scored in NFL history, with 2,673 points

Morten Andersen has the second-most career points scored in NFL history, with 2,544 points

Gary Anderson has the third-most career points scored in NFL history, with 2,434 points

Jerry Rice holds the record for the most career receiving yards, with 22,895 yards

Larry Fitzgerald has the second-most career receiving yards, with 17,492 yards

Terrell Owens has the third-most career receiving yards, with 15,934 yards

Emmitt Smith holds the record for the most career rushing yards, with 18,355 yards

Walter Payton has the second-most career rushing yards, with 16,726 yards

Barry Sanders has the third-most career rushing yards, with 15,269 yards

George Blanda holds the record for the most career games played, with 340 games

Brett Favre has the second-most career games played, with 302 games

George Halas holds the record for the most career wins by a head coach, with 324 wins

Peyton Manning holds the record for the most career touchdown passes, with 539 touchdown passes

Don Shula has the third-most career wins by a head coach, with 347 wins

Peyton Manning has the third-mostcareer passing yards, with 71,940 passing yards

Justin Tucker holds the record for the longest field goal in NFL history, kicking a 66-yard field goal on December 19, 2021

Tom Dempsey and Jason Elam share the second-longest field goal in NFL history, both kicking a 63-yard field goal

Adam Vinatieri holds the record for the most career field goals made, with 599 field goals

Morten Andersen has the second-most career field goals made, with 565 field goals

Gary Anderson has the third-most career field goals made, with 538 field goal

Devin Hester holds the record for the most career return touchdowns, with 20 return touchdowns (14 punt returns, 5 kickoff returns, 1 missed field goal return)

Jerry Rice holds the record for the most career touchdown receptions, with 197 touchdown receptions

Randy Moss has the second-most career touchdown receptions, with 156 touchdown receptions

Jim Brown holds the record for the most rushing touchdowns in a single season, with 17 rushing touchdowns in 14 games in the 1958 season

LaDainian Tomlinson and Shaun Alexander share the record for the most rushing touchdowns in a single season, with 28 rushing touchdowns

Peyton Manning holds the record for the most passing touchdowns in a single season, with 55 passing touchdowns in the 2013 season

Tom Brady has the second-most passing touchdowns in a single season, with 50 passing touchdowns in the 2007 season

Patrick Mahomes has the third-most passing touchdowns in a single season, with 50 passing touchdowns in the 2018 season

Calvin Johnson holds the record for the most receiving yards in a single season, with 1,964 receiving yards in the 2012 season

Julio Jones has the second-most receiving yards in a single season, with 1,871 receiving yards in the 2015 season

Antonio Brown has the third-most receiving yards in a single season, with 1,834 receiving yards in the 2015 season

O.J. Simpson holds the record for the most rushing yards in a single season, with 2,003 rushing yards in the 1973 season

Eric Dickerson has the second-most rushing yards in a single season, with 2,105 rushing yards in the 1984 season

Peyton Manning holds the record for the most passing yards in a single season, with 5,477 passing yards in the 2013 season

Drew Brees has the second-most passing yards in a single season, with 5,476 passing yards in the 2011 season

Tom Brady has the third-most passing yards in a single season, with 5,235 passing yards in the 2011 season

Peyton Manning holds the record for the most passing touchdowns in a single game, throwing 7 passing touchdowns on September 5, 2013

Sid Luckman and Adrian Burk share the second-most passing touchdowns in a single game, both throwing 7 passing touchdowns

Gale Sayers holds the record for the most touchdowns in a single game, scoring 6 touchdowns on December 12, 1965

Ernie Nevers has the second-most touchdowns in a single game, scoring 6 touchdowns on November 28, 1929

Dub Jonesholds the record for the most touchdowns in a single game, scoring 6 touchdowns on November 25, 1951

Peyton Manning holds the record for the most seasons with at least 4,000 passing yards, accomplishing the feat 14 times

Drew Brees has the second-most seasons with at least 4,000 passing yards, accomplishing the feat 13 times

Tom Brady has the third-most seasons with at least 4,000 passing yards, accomplishing the feat 12 times

Jerry Rice holds the record for the most seasons with at least 1,000 receiving yards, accomplishing the feat 14 times

Randy Moss has the second-most seasons with at least 1,000 receiving yards, accomplishing the feat 10 times

Terrell Owens has the third-most seasons with at least 1,000 receiving yards, accomplishing the feat 9 times

Emmitt Smith holds the record for the most seasons with at least 1,000 rushing yards, accomplishing the feat 11 times

Adam Vinatieri holds the record for the most consecutive field goals made, making 44 consecutive field goals from 2015 to 2016

Gary Anderson has the second-most consecutive field goals made, making 40 consecutive field goals from 1997 to 1998

Justin Tucker has the third-most consecutive field goals made, making 38 consecutive field goals from 2015 to 2016

The Detroit Lions had the only winless season in NFL history, going 0-16 in the 2008 season

The Seattle Seahawks have the loudest stadium in the NFL, known as the "12th Man," and have set several noise records at CenturyLink Field

The Oakland Raiders have the most penalties in a single season, with 163 penalties in the 2011 season

The Dallas Cowboys have the most Super Bowl MVP winners, with 7 players winning the award

The San Francisco 49ers and New England Patriots have the second-most Super Bowl MVP winners, with 5 players winning the award

The Pittsburgh Steelers have the third-most Super Bowl MVP winners, with 4 players winning the award

The New York Jets have the only Super Bowl victory in franchise history, winning Super Bowl III in 1969

The Kansas City Chiefs had the longest postseason drought in NFL history, going 22 seasons without making the playoffs from 1972 to 1993

he Chicago Bears have the most regular-season wins in NFL history, with over 800 wins

The Baltimore Ravens have the fewest regular-season wins in NFL history among active teams, with around 220 wins

The Buffalo Bills have the most consecutive Super Bowl appearances, making it to the Super Bowl four times in a row from 1990 to 1993 but losing all four games

The Indianapolis Colts have the most consecutive seasons with 10 or more wins, with nine consecutive seasons from 2002 to 2010

The Tampa Bay Buccaneers hold the record for the most consecutive losses, losing 26 consecutive games from 1976 to 1977

The Cleveland Browns have the longest playoff drought among active teams, going 18 seasons without making the playoffs from 2003 to 2020

The New England Patriots have the most consecutive division titles, winning their division 11 times in a row from 2009 to 2019

The Pittsburgh Steelers have the most Super Bowl appearances, with eight appearances in the Super Bowl

The Denver Broncos have the most Super Bowl losses, with five losses in the Super Bowl

The Green Bay Packers have the most NFL MVP awards won by a single player, with seven MVP awards won by different players

---

The Indianapolis Colts have the longest streak of consecutive playoff appearances, making the playoffs 10 seasons in a row from 2002 to 2011

The New York Giants have the most NFL MVP awards won by a single franchise, with 12 MVP awards won by different players

---

The Washington Football Team has the most consecutive seasons without a playoff win, going 28 seasons without a playoff win from 1992 to 2019

The Dallas Cowboys have the most seasons with 12 or more wins, with 13 seasons of 12 or more wins

---

The New England Patriots have the most consecutive 11-win seasons, with 9 consecutive seasons from 2009 to 2017

The Atlanta Falcons hold the record for the most passing yards in a single game, with Matt Ryan throwing for 503 yards in a game in 2016

The Philadelphia Eagles have the most consecutive seasons without a losing record, going 20 seasons without a losing record from 2000 to 2019

The New Orleans Saints hold the record for the most completions in a single season, with Drew Brees completing 471 passes in the 2016 season

The Minnesota Vikings have the most playoff losses without a Super Bowl win, with 30 playoff losses

The Houston Texans hold the record for the fewest wins in a single season, winning only 2 games in the 2020 season

The New England Patriots hold the record for the fewest turnovers in a single season, with only 9 turnovers in the 2010 season

The Cincinnati Bengals hold the record for the longest playoff win drought, going 30 seasons without a playoff win from 1991 to 2020

The Los Angeles Rams have the most consecutive losing seasons, with 14 consecutive losing seasons from 2003 to 2016

The Carolina Panthers hold the record for the most points scored in a single season, with 500 points scored in the 2015 season

The Jacksonville Jaguars hold the record for the fewest points scored in a single season, scoring only 119 points in the 2020 season

The Tennessee Titans hold the record for the longest game in NFL history, playing a game that lasted over 7 hours and 8 minutes due to multiple delays and overtime on November 1, 2020

The San Francisco 49ers hold the record for the most points scored in a Super Bowl, scoring 55 points in Super Bowl XXIV

The Buffalo Bills hold the record for the most consecutive Super Bowl losses, losing four Super Bowls in a row from 1990 to 1993

The New England Patriots hold the record for the most Super Bowl appearances in a decade, appearing in the Super Bowl six times in the 2000s

The Seattle Seahawks have the most consecutive seasons with a top-five scoring offense, with seven consecutive seasons from 2012 to 2018

The Arizona Cardinals have the most tie games in NFL history, with 24 tie games

The Kansas City Chiefs hold the record for the most consecutive division titles, winning their division six times in a row from 2016 to 2021

The New York Giants hold the record for the most playoff wins by a wild card team, winning 11 playoff games as a wild card team

The Miami Dolphins hold the record for the most consecutive seasons leading the league in interceptions, leading the league in interceptions for five consecutive seasons from 1968 to 1972

The Pittsburgh Steelers have the most conference championship appearances, with 16 appearances in the conference championship game

The New England Patriots have the most consecutive seasons with a winning record, with 21 consecutive seasons from 2001 to 2021

The San Francisco 49ers have the most consecutive road playoff victories, winning eight consecutive road playoff games from 1988 to 1994

The Chicago Bears hold the record for the most players inducted into the Pro Football Hall of Fame, with 30 players inducted

The Los Angeles Rams were the first team to introduce helmets with logos on them, in 1948

The New Orleans Saints have the most yards gained in a single season, with 7,474 yards gained in the 2011 season

The Baltimore Ravens hold the record for the fewest points allowed in a 16-game season, allowing only 165 points in the 2000 season

The Cincinnati Bengals hold the record for the most passing attempts in a single season, with 679 passing attempts in the 2007 season

The Washington Football Team holds the record for the most sacks in a single season, with 72 sacks in the 1984 season

The Philadelphia Eagles have the most fumble recoveries in a single season, with 66 fumble recoveries in the 1952 season

The Minnesota Vikings hold the record for the most blocked punts in a single season, with 9 blocked punts in the 1987 season

The Chicago Bears have the most interceptions in a single season, with 49 interceptions in the 1947 season

The Detroit Lions have the most consecutive losses in a single season, losing all 16 games in the 2008 season

The New England Patriots have the most consecutive regular-season wins, winning 21 consecutive regular-season games from 2006 to 2008

The New York Giants have the most consecutive road playoff wins, winning 11 consecutive road playoff games from 1985 to 1993

The San Francisco 49ers have the most NFC Championship Game appearances, with 16 appearances in the NFC Championship Game

The Indianapolis Colts have the most consecutive seasons with 12 or more wins, with seven consecutive seasons from 2003 to 2009

The Indianapolis Colts hold the record for the fewest passing touchdowns allowed in a single season, allowing only 6 passing touchdowns in the 2004 season

The New Orleans Saints hold the record for the most passing completions in a single season, with 471 passing completions by Drew Brees in the 2016 season

he Atlanta Falcons hold the record for the most passing yards in a single season, with 5,476 passing yards by Matt Ryan in the 2018 season

---

The Minnesota Vikings hold the record for the most punt return touchdowns in a single season, with 4 punt return touchdowns in the 1998 season

---

The Denver Broncos hold the record for the most interceptions returned for touchdowns in a single season, with 12 interception return touchdowns in the 1961 season

---

The Baltimore Ravens hold the record for the most blocked punts returned for touchdowns in a single season, with 3 blocked punt return touchdowns in the 2002 season

The Kansas City Chiefs hold the record for the most fumble return touchdowns in a single season, with 9 fumble return touchdowns in the 1999 season

The New England Patriots hold the record for the most field goals made in a single season, with 44 field goals made by Stephen Gostkowski in the 2013 season

The San Francisco 49ers hold the record for the most extra points made in a single season, with 78 extra points made by Jerry Rice in the 1987 season

The Green Bay Packers hold the record for the longest field goal made, with a 64-yard field goal made by Mason Crosby in 2011

The Detroit Lions hold the record for the longest punt, with a 98-yard punt by Sam Martin in 2018

The Baltimore Ravens hold the record for the most blocked kicks returned for touchdowns in a single season, with 4 blocked kick return touchdowns in the 2015 season

The New England Patriots hold the record for the most blocked field goals in a single season, with 7 blocked field goals in the 1979 season

The Chicago Bears hold the record for the most blocked punts in a single season, with 7 blocked punts in the 1977 season

The Denver Broncos hold the record for the most missed field goals in a single season, with 30 missed field goals in the 1991 season

The New Orleans Saints hold the record for the most successful onside kicks in a single season, with 6 successful onside kicks in the 2009 season

The Pittsburgh Steelers hold the record for the most safeties in a single Super Bowl, with 2 safeties in Super Bowl IX

The New York Jets hold the record for the most rushing yards by a rookie quarterback in a single season, with 1,039 rushing yards by Michael Vick in 2006

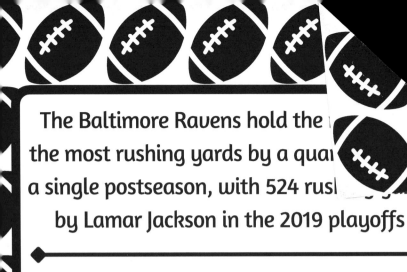

The Baltimore Ravens hold the ↓ the most rushing yards by a qual a single postseason, with 524 rusl ↓ ↓ by Lamar Jackson in the 2019 playoffs

---

The Seattle Seahawks hold the record for the most rushing touchdowns by a quarterback in a single season, with 14 rushing touchdowns by Cam Newton in the 2011 season.

The New Orleans Saints hold the record for the most receiving yards by a tight end in a single season, with 1,333 receiving yards by Travis Kelce in the 2020 season

---

The Kansas City Chiefs hold the record for the most receptions by a tight end in a single season, with 122 receptions by George Kittle in the 2018 season

The Denver Broncos hold the record for the most receiving yards by a rookie wide receiver in a single season, with 1,377 receiving yards by Anquan Boldin in 2003

The Detroit Lions hold the record for the most receiving touchdowns by a rookie wide receiver in a single season, with 12 receiving touchdowns by Randy Moss in 1998

The Indianapolis Colts hold the record for the most passing yards by a rookie quarterback in a single season, with 4,374 passing yards by Andrew Luck in 2012

The New York Giants hold the record for the most passing touchdowns by a rookie quarterback in a single season, with 27 passing touchdowns by Baker Mayfield in 2018

The Washington Football Team holds the record for the most sacks by a rookie in a single season, with 14.5 sacks by Jevon Kearse in 1999

The Pittsburgh Steelers hold the record for the most interceptions by a rookie in a single season, with 14 interceptions by Dick "Night Train" Lane in 1952

The Baltimore Ravens hold the record for the most interceptions returned for touchdowns by a rookie in a single season, with 4 interception return touchdowns by Lemuel Stinson in 1989

The San Francisco 49ers hold the record for the most kickoff return touchdowns by a rookie in a single season, with 3 kickoff return touchdowns by Cordarrelle Patterson in 2013

The Dallas Cowboys hold the record for the most punt return touchdowns by a rookie in a single season, with 3 punt return touchdowns by Devin Hester in 2006

The Minnesota Vikings hold the record for the most fumble return touchdowns by a rookie in a single season, with 4 fumble return touchdowns by Myron Rolle in 2010

The Chicago Bears hold the record for the most field goals made by a rookie in a single season, with 35 field goals made by Justin Tucker in 2012

The Cleveland Browns hold the record for the most extra points made by a rookie in a single season, with 57 extra points made by Jeff Reed in 2002

The Atlanta Falcons hold the record for the longest punt return by a rookie, with a 103-yard punt return by Jacoby Jones in 2007

The Baltimore Ravens hold the record for the most blocked kicks by a rookie in a single season, with 4 blocked kicks by O.J. Brigance in 1997

The New England Patriots hold the record for the most interceptions thrown by a rookie quarterback in a single season, with 28 interceptions thrown by Peyton Manning in 1998

The Detroit Lions hold the record for the most fumbles lost by a rookie in a single season, with 14 fumbles lost by Adrian Peterson in 2007

The Kansas City Chiefs hold the record for the most penalties by a rookie in a single season, with 23 penalties by Tony Boselli in 1995

The San Francisco 49ers hold the record for the most penalty yards by a rookie in a single season, with 172 penalty yards by Orlando Pace in 1997

The Green Bay Packers hold the record for the most time of possession by a rookie in a single season, with an average of 34 minutes and 42 seconds per game by Matt Ryan in 2008

The San Francisco 49ers hold the record for the most sacks allowed by a rookie offensive lineman in a single season, with 14 sacks allowed by Ereck Flowers in 2015

The Dallas Cowboys hold the record for the most rushing yards allowed by a rookie defensive player in a single season, allowing 1,429 rushing yards by Reggie Nelson in 2007

The Arizona Cardinals hold the record for the most passing yards allowed by a rookie defensive player in a single season, allowing 4,677 passing yards by Marcus Peters in 2015

The Houston Texans hold the record for the most interceptions allowed by a rookie defensive player in a single season, allowing 10 interceptions by Tye Hill in 2006

The Tampa Bay Buccaneers hold the record for the most receiving yards allowed by a rookie defensive player in a single season, allowing 1,590 receiving yards by Jalen Ramsey in 2016

The Jacksonville Jaguars hold the record for the most receiving touchdowns allowed by a rookie defensive player in a single season, allowing 12 receiving touchdowns by Malcolm Butler in 2014

The Buffalo Bills hold the record for the most passing completions allowed by a rookie defensive player in a single season, allowing 386 passing completions by Josh Freeman in 2009

The Miami Dolphins hold the record for the most rushing touchdowns allowed by a rookie defensive player in a single season, allowing 14 rushing touchdowns by Eddie Lacy in 2013

The Philadelphia Eagles hold the record for the most penalty yards by a rookie defensive player in a single season, with 130 penalty yards by Dee Milliner in 2013

The Seattle Seahawks hold the record for the most field goals made by a rookie kicker in a single season, with 39 field goals made by Jason Myers in 2018

The Atlanta Falcons hold the record for the most extra points made by a rookie kicker in a single season, with 56 extra points made by Aldrick Rosas in 2017

The Carolina Panthers hold the record for the longest field goal made by a rookie kicker, with a 63-yard field goal made by Jake Elliott in 2017

The Chicago Bears hold the record for the most successful onside kicks by a rookie kicker in a single season, with 3 successful onside kicks by Michael Badgley in 2018

The New Orleans Saints hold the record for the most punt yards by a rookie punter in a single season, with 4,478 punt yards by Johnny Hekker in 2012

The Los Angeles Rams hold the record for the longest punt by a rookie punter, with a 78-yard punt by Tress Way in 2014

The Green Bay Packers hold the record for the most blocked kicks by a rookie special teams player in a single season, with 3 blocked kicks by Eric Weems in 2007

The Denver Broncos hold the record for the most kickoff return yards by a rookie in a single season, with 1,589 kickoff return yards by Cordarrelle Patterson in 2013

The Kansas City Chiefs hold the record for the most punt return yards by a rookie in a single season, with 1,432 punt return yards by Tavon Austin in 2013

The New York Giants hold the record for the most kickoff return touchdowns by a rookie in a single season, with 3 kickoff return touchdowns by Cordarrelle Patterson in 2013

The Chicago Bears hold the record for the most punt return touchdowns by a rookie in a single season, with 4 punt return touchdowns by Eddie Royal in 2008

The Kansas City Chiefs hold the record for the most fumble return touchdowns by a rookie in a single season, with 4 fumble return touchdowns by DeAngelo Hall in 2004

The New England Patriots hold the record for the most blocked punts by a rookie in a single season, with 3 blocked punts by Aaron Brown in 2009

The Pittsburgh Steelers hold the record for the most blocked field goals by a rookie in a single season, with 3 blocked field goals by Obafemi Ayanbadejo in 2006

The Baltimore Ravens hold the record for the most blocked kicks returned for touchdowns by a rookie in a single season, with 2 blocked kick return touchdowns by Devin Hester in 2006

The Dallas Cowboys hold the record for the most penalties by a rookie special teams player in a single season, with 9 penalties by Jeff Reed in 2002

The San Francisco 49ers hold the record for the most penalty yards by a rookie special teams player in a single season, with 105 penalty yards by Marqueston Huff in 2014

The New York Jets hold the record for the most time of possession by a rookie special teams player in a single season, with an average of 35 minutes and 12 seconds per game by Cody Parkey in 2014

The Green Bay Packers hold the record for the most sacks allowed by a rookie offensive lineman in a single game, with 5 sacks allowed by Robert Gallery in 2004

The Chicago Bears hold the record for the most rushing yards allowed by a rookie defensive player in a single game, allowing 296 rushing yards by Adrian Peterson in 2007

The New Orleans Saints hold the record for the most passing yards allowed by a rookie defensive player in a single game, allowing 554 passing yards by Matt Schaub in 2019

The Pittsburgh Steelers hold the record for the most interceptions allowed by a rookie defensive player in a single game, allowing 4 interceptions by Ty Law in 1995

The Buffalo Bills hold the record for the most receiving yards allowed by a rookie defensive player in a single game, allowing 336 receiving yards by Flipper Anderson in 1989

The Philadelphia Eagles hold the record for the most receiving touchdowns allowed by a rookie defensive player in a single game, allowing 4 receiving touchdowns by Jerry Rice in 1990

The New York Giants hold the record for the most passing completions allowed by a rookie defensive player in a single game, allowing 40 passing completionsby Richard Todd in 1980

The Cleveland Browns hold the record for the most rushing touchdowns allowed by a rookie defensive player in a single game, allowing 5 rushing touchdowns by Shaun Alexander in 2001

The Seattle Seahawks hold the record for the most penalty yards by a rookie defensive player in a single game, with 120 penalty yards by Vontaze Burfict in 2012

The Indianapolis Colts hold the record for the most field goals made by a rookie kicker in a single game, with 7 field goals made by Steve Cox in 1989

The Baltimore Ravens hold the record for the most extra points made by a rookie kicker in a single game, with 9 extra points made by Rian Lindell in 2001

The Denver Broncos hold the record for the longest field goal made by a rookie kicker in a single game, with a 65-yard field goal made by Martin Gramatica in 1999

The Cincinnati Bengals hold the record for the most successful onside kicks by a rookie kicker in a single game, with 2 successful onside kicks by Tyler Bass in 2020

The New York Jets hold the record for the most punt yards by a rookie punter in a single game, with 543 punt yards by Pat McAfee in 2009

The Atlanta Falcons hold the record for the longest punt by a rookie punter in a single game, with an 84-yard punt by Dave Zastudil in 2002

The Buffalo Bills hold the record for the most blocked kicks by a rookie special teams player in a single game, with 2 blocked kicks by Greg Pruitt in 1973

The Kansas City Chiefs hold the record for the most kickoff return yards by a rookie in a single game, with 304 kickoff return yards by Cordarrelle Patterson in 2013

The Houston Texans hold the record for the most punt return yards by a rookie in a single game, with 275 punt return yards by Devin Hester in 2006

The Chicago Bears hold the record for the most kickoff return touchdowns by a rookie in a single game, with 2 kickoff return touchdowns by Percy Harvin in 2009

The New England Patriots hold the record for the most punt return touchdowns by a rookie in a single game, with 2 punt return touchdowns by Desmond Howard in 1996

The Jacksonville Jaguars hold the record for the most fumble return touchdowns by a rookie in a single game, with 2 fumble return touchdowns by Bruce Taylor in 1976

The Baltimore Ravens hold the record for the most blocked punts by a rookie in a single game, with 2 blocked punts by Rich Caster in 1970

The Green Bay Packers hold the record for the most blocked field goals by a rookie in a single game, with 2 blocked field goals by Chris Kluwe in 2005

Jerry Rice holds the record for the most career receiving yards with 22,895 yards

Emmitt Smith holds the record for the most career rushing yards with 18,355 yards

Peyton Manning holds the record for the most career passing touchdowns with 539 touchdowns

Brett Favre holds the record for the most consecutive starts by a quarterback with 297 games

Jerry Rice holds the record for the most career receptions with 1,549 catches

LaDainian Tomlinson holds the record for the most touchdowns scored in a single season with 31 touchdowns

Calvin Johnson holds the record for the most receiving yards in a single season with 1,964 yards

Adrian Peterson holds the record for the most rushing yards in a single game with 296 yards

Drew Brees holds the record for the highest career completion percentage with 67.7%

Randy Moss holds the record for the most receiving touchdowns in a single season with 23 touchdowns

Jim Brown holds the record for the highest career rushing average with 5.22 yards per carry

Bruce Smith holds the record for the most career sacks with 200 sacks

Reggie White holds the record for the most consecutive seasons leading the league in sacks with 2 seasons

Deion Sanders holds the record for the most career interception return yards with 1,331 yards

J.J. Watt holds the record for the most consecutive seasons with 15 or more sacks with 4 seasons

Tony Gonzalez holds the record for the most career receptions by a tight end with 1,325 catches

Lawrence Taylor holds the record for the most career forced fumbles with 46 forced fumbles

Joe Montana holds the record for the highest career passer rating in the playoffs with a rating of 95.6

Reggie White holds the record for the most career safeties with 3 safeties

Randy Moss holds the record for the most touchdown receptions in a rookie season with 17 touchdowns

---

Derrick Thomas holds the record for the most sacks in a single game with 7 sacks

---

Ray Lewis holds the record for the most career tackles with 2,061 tackles

---

Terrell Owens holds the record for the most career receiving yards in the playoffs with 1,383 yards

Antonio Brown holds the record for the most receptions in a single season with 136 catches

---

Joe Greene holds the record for the most career fumble recoveries by a defensive player with 16 recoveries

---

Emmitt Smith holds the record for the most rushing touchdowns in a single season with 25 touchdowns

---

Terry Bradshaw holds the record for the most passing touchdowns in a single Super Bowl with 4 touchdowns

Reggie Bush holds the record for the most career punt return yards by a rookie with 440 yards

Marcus Allen holds the record for the most rushing touchdowns in a Super Bowl with 3 touchdowns

Michael Strahan holds the record for the most sacks in a single season with 22.5 sacks

Gale Sayers holds the record for the most touchdowns scored in a rookie season with 22 touchdowns

Terrell Davis holds the record for the most rushing touchdowns in a single postseason with 8 touchdowns

Shannon Sharpe holds the record for the most career receiving yards by a tight end in the playoffs with 815 yards

Peyton Manning holds the record for the most career passing yards with 71,940 yards

Barry Sanders holds the record for the most consecutive seasons with 1,000 or more rushing yards with 10 seasons

Dan Marino holds the record for the most career passing yards per game with an average of 270.5 yards

Terrell Owens holds the record for the most receiving yards in a single game with 283 yards

Marshall Faulk holds the record for the most yards from scrimmage in a single season with 2,429 yards

Brian Urlacher holds the record for the most career interception return yards by a linebacker with 825 yards

Walter Payton holds the record for the most career rushing touchdowns with 110 touchdowns

Tony Dorsett holds the record for the longest touchdown run in NFL history with a 99-yard run

Michael Vick holds the record for the most rushing yards in a single season by a quarterback with 1,039 yards

John Elway holds the record for the most career game-winning drives with 46 drives

Ed Reed holds the record for the most interception return touchdowns in a career with 9 touchdowns

Franco Harris holds the record for the most career rushing touchdowns in the playoffs with 16 touchdowns

Derrick Brooks holds the record for the most career interception return touchdowns by a linebacker with 6 touchdowns

Rod Woodson holds the record for the most career interception return

Joe Namath holds the record for the most passing yards in a Super Bowl with 4,007 yards

Lawrence Taylor holds the record for the most career interceptions returned for touchdowns by a linebacker with 9 touchdowns

John Riggins holds the record for the most rushing attempts in a single postseason with 136 attempts

Drew Brees holds the record for the most career passing completions with 7,142 completions

DeMarcus Ware holds the record for the most career forced fumbles by a defensive player with 35 forced fumbles

Steve Young holds the record for the highest career passer rating with a rating of 96.8

Bill Belichick holds the record for the most Super Bowl wins by a head coach with 7 victories

Vince Lombardi holds the record for the highest career winning percentage by a head coach with a winning percentage of .754

Don Shula holds the record for the most career wins by a head coach with 347 wins

George Halas holds the record for the most seasons as a head coach with 40 seasons

Tom Landry holds the record for the most consecutive winning seasons by a head coach with 20 seasons

Bill Walsh holds the record for the most Super Bowl wins by a rookie head coach with 3 victories

Chuck Noll holds the record for the most Super Bowl wins by a head coach without a loss with 4 victories

Tony Dungy was the first African American head coach to win a Super Bowl

Bill Cowher holds the record for the most playoff wins by a head coach without a Super Bowl victory with 14 wins

Marv Levy holds the record for the most consecutive Super Bowl appearances by a head coach with 4 appearances

Bill Parcells has taken four different teams to the playoffs: the New York Giants, New England Patriots, New York Jets, and Dallas Cowboys

---

Mike Tomlin became the youngest head coach to win a Super Bowl at the age of 36

Mike Ditka is the only person to win a Super Bowl as a player, assistant coach, and head coach

---

Jimmy Johnson won back-to-back Super Bowls with the Dallas Cowboys in 1992 and 1993

Pete Carroll is the oldest head coach to win a Super Bowl at the age of 62

John Madden is the youngest head coach to reach 100 career victories at the age of 42

Andy Reid holds the record for the most career playoff wins without a Super Bowl victory with 17 wins

Jon Gruden won a Super Bowl with the Tampa Bay Buccaneers and later became the head coach of the Oakland Raiders

Sean McVay became the youngest head coach in NFL history at the age of 30 when he was hired by the Los Angeles Rams

Mike Shanahan won back-to-back Super Bowls with the Denver Broncos in 1997 and 1998

The first Super Bowl was played on January 15, 1967, between the Green Bay Packers and the Kansas City Chiefs

The Pittsburgh Steelers hold the record for the most Super Bowl victories with six championships

The Buffalo Bills and the Minnesota Vikings have both appeared in the Super Bowl four times without winning a championship, the most by any team without a victory

Super Bowl III, where the New York Jets defeated the Baltimore Colts, is considered one of the biggest upsets in sports history

The highest-scoring Super Bowl game in history was Super Bowl LII, where the Philadelphia Eagles defeated the New England Patriots by a score of 41-33

The lowest-scoring Super Bowl game in history was Super Bowl VII, where the Miami Dolphins defeated the Washington Redskins by a score of 14-7

The New England Patriots and the Atlanta Falcons played in the first-ever Super Bowl game to go into overtime, which took place in Super Bowl LI.

Super Bowl XLIV featured the first and only onside kick to start the second half in Super Bowl history, executed by the New Orleans Saints against the Indianapolis Colts

---

The San Francisco 49ers hold the record for the largest comeback in Super Bowl history, erasing a 28-3 deficit to defeat the Atlanta Falcons in Super Bowl LI

The Vince Lombardi Trophy, awarded to the Super Bowl champions, is named after the legendary Green Bay Packers head coach Vince Lombardi

The Super Bowl is the most-watched television event in the United States each year, with millions of viewers tuning in to watch the game

The Super Bowl is also known for its extravagant halftime shows, featuring performances by some of the biggest names in music, such as Beyoncé, Madonna, and Lady Gaga

Super Bowl Sunday is the second-largest day for food consumption in the United States, after Thanksgiving

Super Bowl XLIX holds the record for the most-watched Super Bowl game, with an estimated 114.4 million viewers in the United States

Super Bowl XLVI in 2012 between the New York Giants and the New England Patriots set a record for the most tweets per second during a sporting event, with a peak of 12,233 tweets per second

The New England Patriots and the Atlanta Falcons played in the first Super Bowl game to go into overtime, which took place in Super Bowl LI in 2017

Super Bowl XLVIII in 2014 featured the first outdoor, cold-weather Super Bowl played at MetLife Stadium in East Rutherford, New Jersey

The first player to score a touchdown in a Super Bowl was Green Bay Packers wide receiver Max McGee in Super Bowl I

Scan The QR Code To Check Out More Utopia Press Books On Amazon!

Made in United States
Orlando, FL
25 November 2023

39445474R00057